Your
Job
Search

P P Gaudet
M Estier
E Riera

KOGAN PAGE

Kogan Page is the UK member of the Euro Business Publishing Network.
The European members are:
Les Editions d'Organisation, France; Verlag Moderne Industrie, Germany;
Liber, Sweden; Franco Angeli, Italy; and Deusto, Spain.
The Network has been established in response to the growing demand for
international business information and to make the work of Network authors
available in other European languages.

Les Editions d'Organisation, 1992
Translated by Ann Leonard
Illustrated by Sool Sbiera

First published in France in 1992 by
Les Editions d'Organisation, 26 avenue Emile-Zola, 75015 Paris,
entitled Vous et .... la Recherche de Votre Emploi, ISBN 2-7081-1462-X

This edition first published in Great Britain in 1993 by
Kogan Page Ltd, 120 Pentonville Road, London Nl 9JN.

British Library Cataloguing in Publication Data.
A CIP record for this book is available from the British Library.

ISBN 0 7494 1045 0

DTP for Kogan Page by
Jeff Carter 197 South Croxted Road, London SE21 8AY

Printed in Great Britain by
Biddles Ltd, Guildford and Kings Lynn

TABLE OF CONTENTS

The following symbols are used throughout this book to indicate:

Find your way.

Fill it in.

Case Study
THE TURNER FAMILY

Oliver Turner at 19 has just left technical college. He left school when he was 16 and chose a course in mechanics at his local technical college. In his spare time he took driving lessons and passed his driving test on his first attempt, at the age of 17.

He soon realized that he really enjoyed driving and road transport. In fact this, together with his diploma in mechanics, should be enough to enable him to get a job. After registering with his local JobCentre Oliver decides to consult the small ads if he can't manage to get any information from a friend of his who works for a haulage firm.

What procedure should he follow?

Since he left technical college, Oliver realizes that the way he has tackled his job search plan hasn't been very effective. He knows little about job application techniques or follow-up procedures.

In fact who has he written to?

Which companies appeal to him?

It has already been suggested to him that his level of education isn't high enough to be of interest to any prospective employer.

In general he is getting the message that he doesn't have enough experience and that he's too young to hold down a position of responsibility. However, looking around him Oliver sees that there are other young people, also holders of a BTEC diploma, who are already in jobs at the age of 19.

By nature optimistic, he is not discouraged and his objective now is to plan an effective job search strategy.

In any case his sister is older and more qualified than he is, and isn't she in the same boat?

It's September and **Veronica** completed her degree course in communications in June.

Highly motivated, she replies to several job ads but the response is poor and all negative.

Of course the school holiday period hasn't favoured the situation and she hopes that by September employers should be in a more receptive frame of mind.

Veronica is in the habit of scouring the newspapers, especially *The Times*, but even there the ads she comes across aren't exactly tailor made for her.

She is disappointed but conscientiously replies to them anyway: in college weren't they always being told that communications is an ever-expanding sector?

For this reason she is writing off on spec to large British and even foreign organizations.

After all, with her ability to speak French and Spanish she ought to try her luck!

It is, however, the ads in *Media Week* or the *Guardian* on Mondays which send her off into a day-dream, seeing herself in positions like 'Head of Public Relations for an international organization' – 'Responsible for internal communication in a large American bank' – 'Human Resources Assistant in charge of training in a large holding company'.

In emphasizing her four years of study she is aware of having learned a

lot but in real terms, what can she do? Hers is not an isolated case; many young people of her age, straight out of university, experience great difficulty in taking the first steps into the world of work.

As holder of a degree which is highly prized in the eyes of the university world, Veronica refuses to be discouraged, unlike her mother Nicole.

Now that her third child is at school **Nicole** is considering a return to the workforce. But to someone who hasn't clocked in for 15 years the market seems very different. Gone are the days when the evening papers published job offers and all you had to do was turn up to be offered the job on the spot.

The role of 'data processor' has certainly changed. The term itself has all but disappeared. So what classification and what publication should she consult?

Nicole is all geared up to the idea of a return to work which represents for her a real role in society. Having seen her three children through school she now wants to develop an interest independent of the home. As secretary of the local Women's Group she regularly uses her typing and organizational skills as well as holding a position of responsibility.

These factors all lead her to consider a secretarial post and it is over such ads that she lingers. From office worker to varying secretarial positions, all ads stipulate a working knowledge of word processor and computer skills. On top of all this, in spite of the positive encouragement from her professional adviser at the JobCentre she feels alone and lacking in direction.

Does her age, 44, count against her? Certainly the employment market can be a complicated area.

What must she highlight in order to her improve her chances as a candidate ? How should she approach a company? On the advice of her daughter she has revised her CV but is that enough? Maybe she should consider doing a full-time training course in secretarial and word processing skills ?

Her husband **John**, seems to be stuck at the same point: he is unaware of the new techniques involved in finding a job. At 46, having spent 19 years working for a plastics firm as shop foreman, John is considering working for another company. It's a question for him of making the most of his experience and qualities in a small/medium-sized company where he would earn more money and enjoy greater status. He is an expert in his own field and is familiar with the most up-to-date technology. He supervises and motivates a team of six people and he is also used to dealing with representatives from other companies. However, he now feels he is at a turning point in his career and must make arrangements for his own professional development. Having consulted several career management manuals he is aware that he must plan a very specific strategy.

But he doesn't feel completely prepared. He has to sell himself and his main difficulty is in taking stock of his career, his qualities and even his objectives. After that, how does he present himself to a small/medium-sized company?

Wanting to move closer to home: is that a good argument to present to a prospective employer?

John doesn't know when is the right time to launch himself on to the job market and is reflecting on the compilation of a dossier which would be of interest to a small/medium-sized company.

Apart from the particular case of the Turner family, we will examine several different types of job search and define the techniques necessary for dealing with each. The themes we will deal with have already arisen in the stories of the Turners and we will follow them on their search for work. Let's hope that the case of this family will help you to organize your own job search strategy.

Section 1
EVALUATION

SELF-ASSESSMENT TEST A

Is your job search unsuccessful?
Place a tick in the box corresponding to your answer and count one point for each 'likely' answer.

	LIKELY	UNLIKELY
1 You seem to come across very few ads which concern you.		
2 You never quite meet the job requirements stated in terms of age, training or location.		
3 You don't really know what job to apply for.		
4 The question 'What can you do?' makes you nervous.		
5 The job market is changing and you no longer know what classification you come under.		
6 You are ready to accept a job demanding the minimum qualifications.		
7 There seems to be less demand for your type of work.		
8 You specialize in one area and one area only.		

TOTAL A
(likely)

RESULTS OF TEST A

0 - 3 POINTS

Your professional profile is complete. You could still add a few finishing touches but that isn't where the main problem lies. Continue with the self-assessment testing to detect the reasons for the failure in your job search efforts.

3 - 6 POINTS

Your professional profile needs to be further developed. Reconsider your objectives and pay particular attention to the type of career person you are. Widen the scope of your search, define your aptitudes and discover all the functions you are capable of carrying out.

6 - 8 POINTS

Watch out, you can't get a job without knowing what you really want or can do. Carefully revise your professional profile.
No test can be undertaken without proper preparation. The rest will follow automatically.

SELF-ASSESSMENT TEST B

	LIKELY	UNLIKELY
1 You have officially been looking for a job for more than a year.	....	....
2 You feel you are too old or, more precisely, employers think you're too old.	....	....
3 You have no experience.	....	....
4 You have no problem finding ads, you get called to a few interviews but nothing ever comes of it.	....	....
5 You know what you want to do but you can never find an ad relating to your field.	....	....
6 You might have found something but it didn't really suit you after all (hours, distance, location etc).	....	....
7 Basically, your job has changed and your skills are out of date and you are well aware of it.	....	....
8 You have actually chosen a few ads but you don't know where to go from there.	....	....

TOTAL B
(likely)

RESULTS OF TEST B

0 - 3 POINTS
Good, you are just two steps away from that job. Are you examining all sources of job leads? Read carefully through Section 4 'Devising a strategy'.

3 - 6 POINTS
You are not in control of your job search situation.
All is not yet lost, there is opportunity for everyone. Be positive and continue with your self-assessment.

6 - 8 POINTS
In order to find a job, set out your objectives.
Week 1 : Complete your personal and professional profiles.
Week 2 : Check out all leads, prepare your correspondence and interview technique. Go into action.
Week 3 : Increase your exposure by setting yourself the target of 20 applications a week; answering ads and applications on spec.

Don't rely on luck or chance alone when looking for a job, but on yourself, on your work and your method.

LET'S GET OUR TERMINOLOGY RIGHT

Recruiters, career guidance counsellors and seasoned job searchers all have a basic common vocabulary. Here are a few definitions which should help to clear up any misunderstandings.

Aptitudes, skills, qualities...

FUNCTION: the role and purpose you fulfil in a company.

TASKS: the work or activity that has to be carried out.

APTITUDES: natural or acquired knowledge and ability to do something.

SKILLS: extended knowledge or expertise in an area (formally recognized).

QUALITIES: personal assets or merit, favourable character traits.

EXERCISE 1

EVALUATION CHART

Fill this in as accurately as possible.
Get help in doing so if necessary.

TITLE OF JOB OR ACTIVITY WITHIN THE LAST FIVE YEARS	FUNCTION	TASKS CARRIED OUT	APTITUDES	QUALITIES NECESSARY

•
YOUR PROFESSIONAL PROFILE
• •

Before undertaking your job search do a quick check-up. The parachutist always checks his equipment before jumping. The showjumper always verifies the safety of his mount before heading for the fences.

Out of the blue, Nicole was given the awkward assignment of defining her professional profile. Here's her reply:

'As mother to three children, I gave up working in order to look after them. Before that I was a secretary, but I've never used a word processor. Now I'm available for work. I'm looking for a post perhaps as a receptionist or a secretary.....'

WHAT DO YOU THINK?

What image of herself does Nicole present to us?
She makes a distinction between her current position and her past one as if she no longer feels that she is a secre-

tary. Word processing isn't the only thing a secretary has to be able to do. Does she convey her aptitudes? No. Does she convey her skills? No. Would you be convinced enough by her presentation to employ her?

LET'S GO BACK OVER NICOLE'S PRESENTATION, USING THE SAME INSTRUCTIONS.

'As a trained secretary, I have not exercised my professional activity for some years. I've put these years to good use working voluntarily for a children's judo club as secretary and organizer. I organized meetings and outings and dealt with the parents of the pupils. I was also in charge of registration, monitoring attendance and typing correspondence. I took an active role at meetings concerning the club, the membership rate of which has tripled in the last five years. Now my availability and sense of responsibility allow me to place my experience at the service of a company.'

PERSONAL CONCLUSION

A good presentation must be positive and should, above all, serve to highlight your personal and professional aptitudes.

Nicole has revised her presentation. What about you?
How would you go about putting your presentation together?

Think about the image you project of yourself.
Give an account of your skills and aptitudes in ten lines.

Personal observations

Section 2
PERSONAL PROFILE

WHAT'S THE PURPOSE OF A PERSONAL PROFILE?

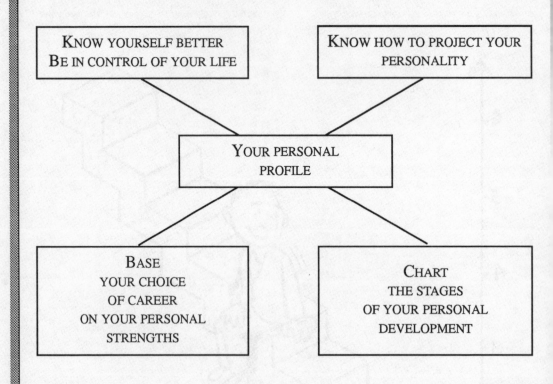

KNOW YOURSELF BETTER
BE IN CONTROL OF YOUR LIFE

KNOW HOW TO PROJECT YOUR
PERSONALITY

YOUR PERSONAL
PROFILE

BASE
YOUR CHOICE
OF CAREER
ON YOUR PERSONAL
STRENGTHS

CHART
THE STAGES
OF YOUR PERSONAL
DEVELOPMENT

WHO AM I?

What are your personal qualities? What are the strengths and weaknesses of your personality? These questions are often asked during a job interview. It's not so easy to be objective about them.

We'll supply you with a preliminary guideline, just read on. It will help you to construct a career plan. Success in your career depends on both your aptitudes and your temperament.

TEST 1

Answer the following four lists of questions. Place an X in the box corresponding to your behaviour. Total your score at the end of each list and multiply the number of replies by the number at the top of each column.

List no 1. A sense of the practical

	NEVER 0	SOME-TIMES 1	OFTEN 3	VERY OFTEN 6
Do you like DIY?				
Do you practise a sport?				
Can you repair things?				
Can you manage your own expenditure?				
Do you have a sense of direction?				
Do you ever play a game of skill?				
Do you look after your body?				
Number of replies per column				
Column total (multiply the number of replies in each column by the number at the top of the column)		+	+	+
Total score for list no 1 (the sum of the figures on the previous line)				=

TEST 2

List no 2. Do you take care of yourself?

	NEVER	SOME-TIMES	OFTEN	VERY OFTEN
	0	1	3	6
Do you like to spend time on your own?				
Are you in control of your emotions?				
Do you worry about what other people think of you?				
Do you take time to reflect on your behaviour in the past?				
Do you have confidence in yourself?				
Do you ever talk about your problems?				
Number of replies per column				
Column total (multiply the number of replies in each column by the number at the top of the column)		+	+	+
Total score for list no 2 (the sum of the figures on the previous line)			=	

TEST 3

List no 3. Reflection, is that your thing?

	NEVER 0	SOME-TIMES 1	OFTEN 3	VERY OFTEN 6
Do you think before you act?				
Do you read the daily or weekly newspapers?				
Do you ever read a book?				
Do you ever just listen to music without doing something else at the same time?				
Do you attach any importance to the means you employ to obtain an end result?				
Do you ever write? To friends, for yourself or for publication?				
Do you like to argue about values and principles?				
Number of replies per column				
Column total (multiply the number of replies in each column by the number at the top of the column)		+	+	+
Total score for list no 3 (the sum of the figures on the previous line)			=	

TEST 4

List no 4. Are you at ease with others?

	NEVER	SOME-TIMES	OFTEN	VERY OFTEN
	0	1	3	6
Do your friends talk to you about themselves?				
Do you give presents?				
Do you face up to a conflict?				
Do you dare to ask for what you want?				
When you are talking to somebody do you ever refer to the relationship you have with that person?				
Do you like meeting new faces?				
If somebody asks you in person to do something for them would you dare refuse?				
Number of replies per column				
Column total (multiply the number of replies in each column by the number at the top of the column)		+	+	+
Total score for list no 4 (the sum of the figures on the previous line)			=	

ANALYSIS OF YOUR RESULTS
DETERMINE YOUR AREA

Place the total from each list in the corresponding box on the chart.

	LIST NO 1 A sense of the practical	LIST NO 2 Do you take care of your- self?	LIST NO 3 Reflection	LIST NO 4 At ease with others
Your scores				
	A as in Action	I as in Introvert	R as in Reflection	E as in Extrovert

A *is your dominant score*

You love action, you need to be the centre of your universe. You run the risk of being very dissatisfied with a job too closely centred around study or research, where you can't see immediate results from your work.

I *is your dominant score*

You are totally at ease with yourself. So much so that you have no problem working alone on a project for which you have complete responsibility. Jobs which involve teamwork to a large extent, dealing with clients or partners, are not for you.

R *is your dominant score*

You tend to shy away from the type of work that involves spontaneous action. You prefer to understand how things work in order to be able to propose improvements or forecast problems and thereby devise productive working methods. You prefer to conceptualize. Jobs which involve a succession of tasks to be carried out will only put you off.

E *is your dominant score*

You like human contact, working with others and negotiation. Don't settle for a job which would involve working alone and deprive you of the outside stimulation you desire.

VERONICA'S STORY

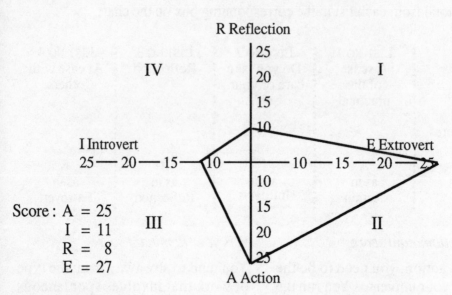

Score : A = 25
I = 11
R = 8
E = 27

Centre of gravity
Axis RA = 8.5
Axis IE = 8

Commentary

Veronica's centre of gravity places her in quadrant II (action, extrovert). She is an extrovert, and has a taste for action. On the other hand, introversion and reflection aren't really her cup of tea.

She runs the risk of not doing herself justice in highly intellectual or solitary jobs. She would become bored doing technical, artistic or scientific work.

The profession which would best suit her personality must incorporate an element of the practical and also allow her to be in constant contact with others.

The test confirms her direction towards the communication sector for which she has already acquired the necessary skills, thanks to her university course.

CHART YOUR AIRE

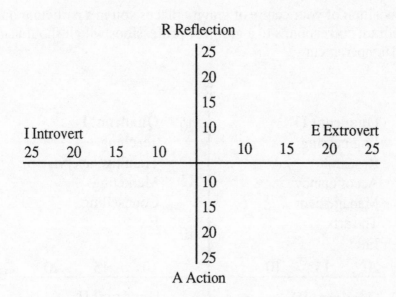

☞ Calculate your centre of gravity G and draw it on to your AIRE

– on the axis RA (numbers scored) $\dfrac{R - A}{2}$ = ⬚

– on the axis IE (numbers scored) $\dfrac{I - E}{2}$ = ⬚

ONE STEP FURTHER

☞ The position of your centre of gravity places you in a particular quadrant. Each quadrant corresponds to a group of professions which should suit your skills and temperament.

R

Quadrant IV	20 **Quadrant I**
Engineering	Teaching
Research	Training/supervision
Accountancy	15 Marketing
Management	Counselling
The arts	Etc
Etc	10

I   20   15   10   10   15   20   E

Quadrant III	**Quadrant II**
Arts and crafts	10 Sales
Technician	Reception
Operator	Secretarial
Tradesman	15 Health and social
Etc	sectors
	Etc
	20

A

PERSONAL CONCLUSION

In the light of this first draft profile and all you know about yourself, identify your main assets, your weak points and your stages of personal development.

MY THREE MAIN ASSETS:

1...

2...

3...

MY THREE WEAK POINTS:

1...

2...

3...

THE QUALITIES I WOULD LIKE TO DEVELOP:

1...

2...

3...

Personal observations

Section 3
CAREER PLAN

THE FAMILY BACKGROUND

Whether you're aware of it or not the professions of your parents and grandparents have had and will continue to have a profound influence on your choice of direction. The object of this exercise is to give you an insight into the reasons behind your choice of profession.

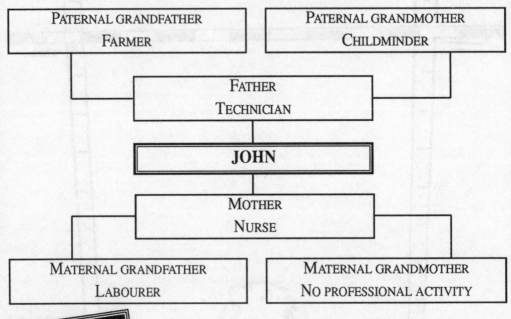

PATERNAL GRANDFATHER	PATERNAL GRANDMOTHER
FARMER	CHILDMINDER

FATHER
TECHNICIAN

JOHN

MOTHER
NURSE

MATERNAL GRANDFATHER	MATERNAL GRANDMOTHER
LABOURER	NO PROFESSIONAL ACTIVITY

Role and influence of family background: after thinking about it, John realizes that his parents have implanted in him the idea that a proper and regular job will bring its own rewards. It would thus appear that this is the underlying motivation for his career to date. He has given a lot to his job and has slowly but surely moved up through the ranks of the same company. Now, although he intends to hold on to these family values, he finds it is not enough to satisfy him. He's now faced with a new situation where he must market his skills and expertise.

THE FAMILY ALBUM

FILL IN THE BOXES INDICATING THE JOBS HELD
BY THE VARIOUS MEMBERS OF YOUR FAMILY

PATERNAL GRANDFATHER	PATERNAL GRANDMOTHER

FATHER

YOU

MOTHER

MATERNAL GRANDFATHER	MATERNAL GRANDMOTHER

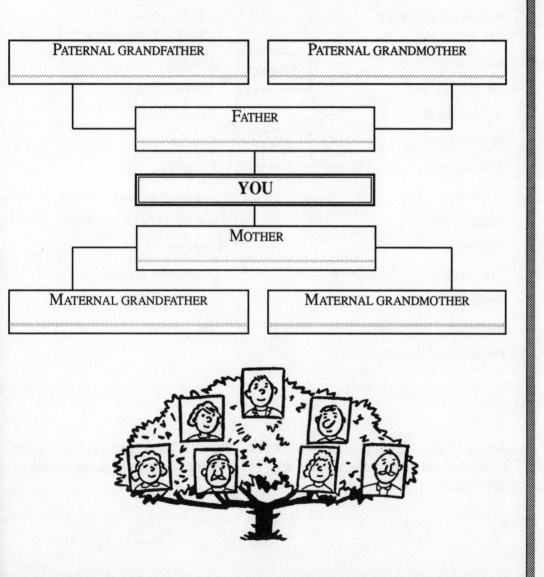

33

CONCLUSION

We have tried to gain an insight into the wishes of John's parents for his future.

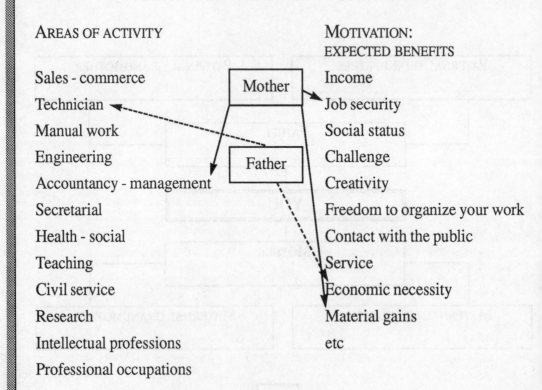

AREAS OF ACTIVITY

Sales - commerce
Technician
Manual work
Engineering
Accountancy - management
Secretarial
Health - social
Teaching
Civil service
Research
Intellectual professions
Professional occupations

Mother

Father

MOTIVATION:
EXPECTED BENEFITS

Income
Job security
Social status
Challenge
Creativity
Freedom to organize your work
Contact with the public
Service
Economic necessity
Material gains
etc

John's chart integrated all the wishes of his parents: his current post combines technical and management activities. He is trying to transmit these values to his children.

AND WHAT ABOUT YOU?

What profession would your parents have wished for you? Why?

Link the activity areas on the left with the reasons given on the right. You may add to these lists if necessary.

Sales - commerce	Income
Technical	Job security
Manual work	Social status
Engineering	Challenge
Accountancy - management	Creativity
Secretarial	Freedom to organize
Health and social	Contact with the public
Teaching	Service
Civil service	Economic necessity
Research	Material gains
Intellectual professions	etc
Professional occupations	

☞ At the moment my job is ....

☞ I chose this job because...

☞ The values it incorporates are...

☞ And I hope to pass them on to...

THE IDEAL PROFESSIONS

JOHN TURNER'S LIFELINE: THE SUCCESSION OF PROFESSIONS HE DREAMED ABOUT

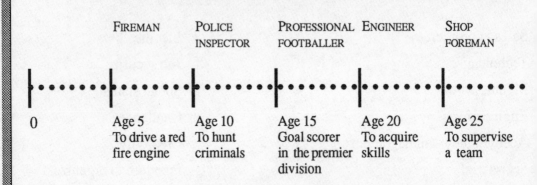

	FIREMAN	POLICE INSPECTOR	PROFESSIONAL FOOTBALLER	ENGINEER	SHOP FOREMAN
0	Age 5 To drive a red fire engine	Age 10 To hunt criminals	Age 15 Goal scorer in the premier division	Age 20 To acquire skills	Age 25 To supervise a team

What John remembers of his dreams of childhood and as a young man:
'The recurring element in these dreams: I'm always on the go, I want to see the results of my work, I want to become more and more efficient, to be in control. Furthermore, I really like supervising and being recognized as a capable person. Certainly at the age of 20, there was no limit to my aspirations and I dreamed of becoming an engineer. However, I'm now at a turning point where I want to begin a new stage and take my career in hand.'

YOUR LIFELINE

☞ Do you remember the jobs that attracted you as a child, adolescent or young adult. In the boxes above your lifeline insert the titles of these jobs and underneath the reasons why they appealed to you.

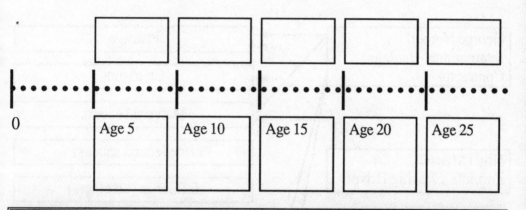

0

Age 5   Age 10   Age 15   Age 20   Age 25

Personal observations

What remains of those dreams today?
What would you still like to achieve?

THE PROFESSIONALS YOU ADMIRE

Oliver, like all of us, has two role models in the professional world: Nigel Mansell and George Norbert, the father of a friend.
This is what he admires about them:

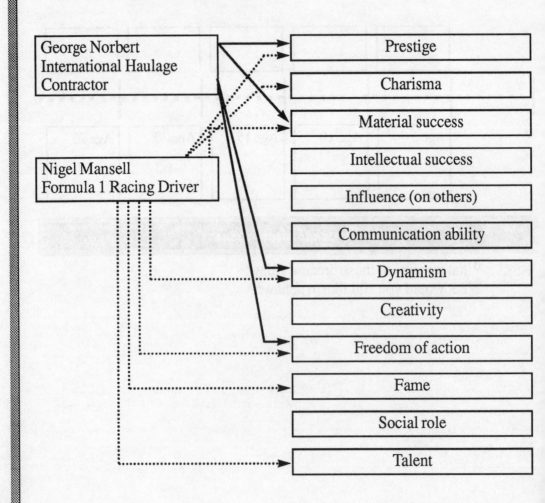

☞ Note in the left-hand column as they come into your head, the names of any professionals you admire whether famous people or personal acquaintances.

Link the name to the characteristics that you admire most in them.

But why?

	Prestige
	Charisma
	Material success
	Intellectual success
	Influence (on others)
	Communication ability
	Dynamism
	Creativity
	Freedom of action
	Fame
	Social role
	Talent

☞ Pick out three values that you would like to have associated with your work.

THEORY OF MOTIVATION

A good recruiter knows that the motivations of employees must reflect the interests of his company.

In order to be more convincing and to feel more fulfilled you have to try to satisfy your motivations.

An American psycho-sociologist, Abraham Maslow, charted professional motivations in ascending order in the shape of a pyramid. As soon as one fundamental need is fulfilled, it disappears and is replaced by one of a higher calibre. At the summit of the pyramid is the desire to be fulfilled by your professional life.

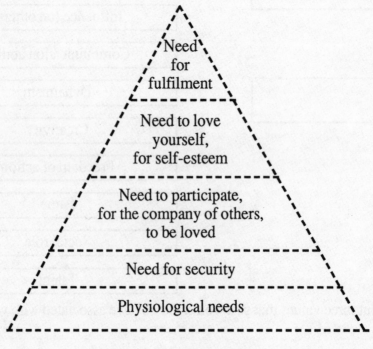

Maslow's pyramid of needs

WHAT MOTIVATES YOU

Reply spontaneously to the questions below:

YOU WANT TO WORK	NOT REALLY SCORE 0	MORE OR LESS SCORE 3	ABSOLUTELY SCORE 5
1 To bring home a salary, or have a second salary			
2 For the security of a regular job			
3 To fulfil a dream or to achieve independence			
4 To be well thought of by others and by yourself			
5 Insurance for the future (a job = a wage)			
6 So you won't feel alone			
7 To pay the bills but also to leave you free time for leisure activities			
8 For self-development and to take on responsibility			
9 To work with a good team			
10 To achieve personal well-being and harmony			
11 To go on learning			
12 To remain active			
13 To maintain a certain standard of living			
14 To feel useful throughout the day			
15 To be able to treat yourself to extras (house, car)			

Transfer your scores to the table on page 42.

ANALYSIS OF THE RESULTS

ANALYSIS OF RESULTS

A		B		C		D		E	
Q	Score	Q	Score	Q	Score	Q	Score	Q	Score
1		2		3		4		8	
7		5		6		12		10	
14		15		9		13		11	
Total		Total		Total		Total		Total	

MOSTLY A: PHYSIOLOGICAL NEEDS

You need to work for material reasons.

☞ Broaden your search. Widen your scope of activities, be more versatile. Make your approaches to companies in person.

MOSTLY B: NEED FOR SECURITY

Having a salary and a steady job will reassure you above all else.

☞ Sit for open examinations; have you considered:
– the civil service, the post office, going down in person to your local council, contacting hospitals etc.

MOSTLY C: NEED TO PARTICIPATE

You like to work in a team and are sensitive to group atmosphere. You need to feel useful...

☞ Pay attention to areas of communication:
– personalize your written correspondence, be selective and increase your on spec applications, be especially attentive during interviews...

MOSTLY D: NEED FOR SELF-RESPECT

You will only blossom with the support and recognition of others.

☞ During an interview, be quite certain of your goal, where you are going to fit in. Ensuring that your personality fits in with the professional culture is more important than your ability to do the work.

MOSTLY E: NEED FOR PROFESSIONAL FULFILMENT

You want to apply your skills to their best possible advantage and you have a desire to achieve something.

☞ Go for it !

Improvise, be practical, make proposals, have meetings with organizations. Listen to what they have to say and act accordingly. Don't allow your job description to make you sound less than versatile or limited. Attend open days in order to understand the expectations of different organizations.

YOUR GRAPH

Record your own scores from A, B, C, D and E from the previous page on to the graph below to gain an insight into your own motivating factors.

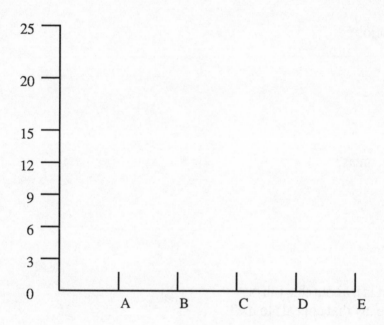

PERSONAL CONCLUSION

Next, in order to compile my CV, my correspondence and, in particular, to support my interview technique, I need to plan my line of argument.

It must be to the point, concise and effective, so I can always justify it.

My career plan is shaped like this:

☞ What job?

☞ What areas?

☞ What is it about this job or company that appeals to me?

☞ On a personal level what do I hope to gain from this job?

Section 4
DEVISING A STRATEGY

ORDER OF PRIORITIES

A. Once you have clearly identified your personal goals and objectives, you must lay out a series of steps to follow which will constitute the job search strategy you are about to implement.

The list of priorities which you will identify on p47 will help you to target more easily those companies which you are going to approach.

Bear in mind two objectives from this chapter:

1. To create my strategy, that is to say, my plan to launch myself on the job market.

2. To compile a list of companies which correspond to my needs and which will be the target points for my job search scheme.

B. In order to specify your main priorities it is crucial to appreciate these three stages:

1. To examine the criteria and mark them on a personal rating from 0 to 10 (p47);

2. Select your top three and examine the consequences that arise from such a choice (p48);

3. Base your search on these three, incorporating the other elements in order to complete the picture.

Obviously these elements will determine your final choice, tipping the balance in favour of a particular position.

C. Now that you have clarified your order of priorities what's the next move? (p49)

In Veronica's case her top priority is to have a series of interesting and varied duties to perform.

She would also like to follow a training programme.

So she intends to target the small to medium-range businesses, emphasizing her age, and ask for a contract which includes a training clause.

She will therefore consult the local press and choose ads which stipulate the provision of in-house training.

YOUR PRIORITIES GRAPH

Each of us has his own deciding factors. We have selected ten. Rate each one in order of importance by giving each a mark between 0 and 10 (0 being the lowest score).
Draw your graph.
It is the basis for ideas and tactics.

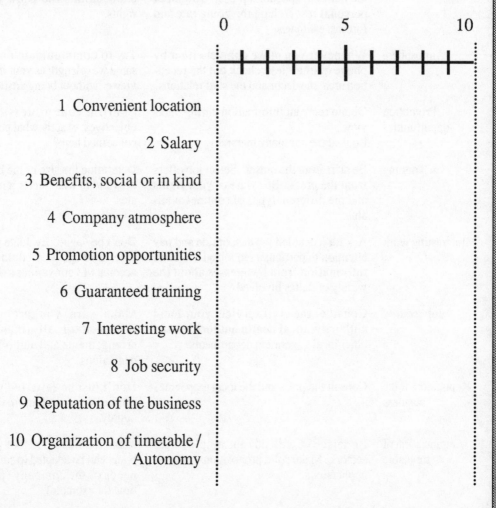

0   5   10

1 Convenient location

2 Salary

3 Benefits, social or in kind

4 Company atmosphere

5 Promotion opportunities

6 Guaranteed training

7 Interesting work

8 Job security

9 Reputation of the business

10 Organization of timetable /
Autonomy

I'M LOOKING FOR	SO I SHOULD	AND ABOVE ALL
Convenient location	Consult the local press for details. Look up the directories and do a tour of the area. Seek information on the local economy (mailing lists, Chamber of Commerce and Industry, local council etc).	Don't get sidetracked. Decide on your area of action based on the number of businesses it contains.
Salary - social or other benefits	Target the larger businesses. Look at the employment conditions on offer. Check the national specialist press. Do a bit of personal research on the going rate and forecast estimates.	Calculate your market value. Be prepared to justify your expectations and know your rights.
Atmosphere	Whenever you make contact either by phone or interview, check out the reception area, the decor and the staff relations.	Try to communicate on the same wavelength as your interviewer without being artificial.
Promotion opportunities	Obtain relevant information during interview. Look at the company hierarchy.	Confirm your professional objectives: exactly what post is concerned here?
Training	Be alert from the outset. Select job offers from the press. Be aware of your rights and the different types of contract available.	Determine the size of the business and in what sector it operates.
Interesting work	Ask for a detailed job description and pay attention to particulars in job ads. Obtain information from businesses about the variety of duties involved.	Don't be vague. Evaluate your role and give a detailed account of your various skills.
Job security	Consider the civil service; your local authority; local health authorities and other local goverment departments.	Make sure you are well informed of all financial arrangements and authorized deductions.
Reputation of the business	Consult the press and the local grapevine.	Don't just be satisfied with rumours; research more thoroughly.
Organization of timetable	Be selective with ads and employment sectors. Make solid propositions, on spec applications.	Make it understood that your hours can be adapted to suit the needs of the company (part-time for example).

YOUR DECIDING FACTORS

And what about you? What are your deciding factors?

I go for:

::

::

::

::

::

I decide therefore to:

::

::

::

::

::

THE EMPLOYMENT MARKET

Tick your initial response.
When I'm looking for a job:

	YES	NO
1 I go to the JobCentre		
2 I read the local paper (or the local free paper)		
3 I go straight to the businesses to establish their needs		
4 I attend open days in companies		
5 I check out the local grapevine (friends, family)		
6 I register with temporary employment agencies		
7 I contact my local careers advice centre		
8 I listen to job offers on the radio		
9 I enter competitions		
10 I write off on spec to companies to offer my services		
11 I use specialist trade publications in my job search		
12 I notify my professional association that I am looking for work		

TOTAL

ANALYSIS OF RESULTS

COUNT UP ALL THE 'YES' REPLIES

9 - 12

Well done! Your search is well under way. If there is no positive outcome, check whether:
- you're heading for the right career (test);
- the organizations you're targeting are well chosen ones;
- you should step up the entire process, your job is waiting at the finish line!

6 - 9

Watch out – you're not using all the job search techniques available to you and you run the risk of missing out. Go over the steps you're not implementing and put them into action.

Less than 6

Even equipped with a good CV, you'll have difficulty finding a job if you don't make a greater effort.
You're taking chances and that's unwise.

THE OPEN MARKET

This is made up of 'visible' job offers:
- Press
- Temporary employment agencies
- JobCentres
- Forums for jobs

It constitutes 30 per cent of all available posts.

THE CLOSED MARKET

This is made up of 'invisible' job offers:
- On spec applications
- Recommendations

It constitutes 70 per cent of all available posts.

THE REGIONAL PRESS

Consult the directories, pick out the names of regional press publications which interest you and take out a subscription or see if they are available at your local library.

For example:

LONDON AND THE SOUTH EAST:
Evening Standard
The Jobpaper
Loot
Midweek
Ms London   — free magazines
Southern Cross
Time Out

OUTSIDE LONDON:
The Belfast Telegraph
Birmingham Evening Mail
Coventry Evening Telegraph
Eastern Daily Press (Norwich)
Glasgow Herald
The Irish Times

Liverpool Echo
The Manchester Evening News
Nottingham Evening Post
The Scotsman
The Western Daily Press (Bristol)
The Yorkshire Post

YOUR CHECK-LIST
COMPLETE IT

DAILY PAPERS
The Daily Mail
The Daily Telegraph
The Express
Financial Times
The Guardian
The Independent
The Times

PROFESSIONAL WEEKLIES
Accountancy Age
The Bookseller
The Lancet
The Law Society's Gazette
New Civil Engineer
Taxation

NATIONAL WEEKLY PUBLICATIONS
The Economist
The Lady
New Statesman & Society
Observer
Spectator

SPECIALIST WEEKLY PUBLICATIONS
Campaign
Nature
New Scientist
Nursing Times
PR Week
Stage and Television Today
Times Educational Supplement
UK Press Gazette

OTHER SOURCES

Most new televisions now have Ceefax and Teletext services which allow the viewer access to all kinds of information. The services and codes are as follows:

BBC1
BBC2 ⎤ advertises job vacancies in the BBC on Ceefax code 696

Channel 4 advertises a range of jobs countrywide on Teletext on 4, Jobfinder Code 649

Can you think of any other sources of information regarding job vacancies in your area?

YOUR PERSONAL FILE

Now you can begin to compile your list of businesses.
Your knowledge of the employment market and your order of priorities will guide you.
Decide which businesses you are going to contact and your method of approach.
Set yourself specific targets, eg: 'I'm going to contact 20 businesses a week...'

NAME OF THE BUSINESS	PERSON YOU SPOKE TO ADDRESS/TELEPHONE NUMBER	WHAT'S THE MOTIVATING FACTOR?

PERSONAL CONCLUSION

I organize my job search with the following priorities in mind:

☞ ....

☞ ....

☞ ....

I visit the JobCentre every:

☞ ....

☞ address ....

I consult the general and specialist press, in particular:

☞ ....

☞ ....

☞ ....

And also the free papers in the area I want to work
(I subscribe if necessary):

☞ ....

☞ ....

☞ ....

What conclusions do you draw about the open market?

....

....

Section 5
CURRICULUM VITAE

SELF-ASSESSMENT TEST

Now let's take a look at your ability to compile an effective CV. Reply honestly to the following statements and then count up the number of Xs in the 'yes' column.

	NO	YES
1 You possess several versions of your CV.	....	....
2 It's quite possible that you have neglected to mention certain details of your career to date.	....	....
3 There are several optional elements in your CV, eg, age, marital status.	....	....
4 The non-compulsory heading 'Other details', completes your CV.	....	....
5 A caption adds a little extra personal touch to a CV.	....	....
6 A photograph, especially in the case of an on spec application, is unnecessary.	....	....
7 Under no circumstances is the subject of pay mentioned in a CV.	....	....
8 Whether an experienced or first-time job searcher, your CV should never exceed two pages.	....	....
9 The lay-out and content of a CV are of equal importance.	....	....
10 The CV is a must when looking for a job.	....	....

TOTAL

RESULTS

TO BE CALCULATED ON COMPLETION OF THE
SELF-ASSESSMENT TEST

'YES' 0-3

You seem to be in the dark where CVs are concerned. The only solution would seem to be a fresh start, using the advice given in this chapter. Remember to work on the layout as well as the content.

'YES' 3-6

In general you do know how to put a CV together, but there are still some areas which need improving. You should approach it with the idea that a CV needs to be both convincing and visually impressive.

'YES' 6-10

Well done, the compilation of a CV holds no mysteries for you. You're in firm control and the advice in this chapter only serves to confirm your method.

THE GOLDEN RULES OF A GOOD CV

LAY-OUT: THE FIVE ESSENTIAL POINTS

☞ **1.** Before a prospective employer can read a CV, he has to see it.
As much care must be taken with style, vocabulary, spelling and accuracy as with the printing, presentation and length. You should get a competent third party to proofread your CV for you.
The CV is the first step in your promotional campaign and therefore it should be treated with great care. It is the CV which will create the first impression.

☞ **2.** The length of your CV is not strictly proportional to the length of your career. Try to avoid boring the employer by baring all in your CV. It should be concise and to the point. It should seize the employer's attention and he'll tire easily after more than two pages.

☞ **3.** The inclusion of a photo is strongly advised if the ad demands it. In the case of an on spec application, the choice is yours. Obviously, the photo (or a photocopied one) adds a personal touch especially if the CV has to pass through many hands.
Make sure that you're relaxed and smiling.

☞ **4.** A caption is a desirable extra in a CV. It makes it more personal and also serves to highlight whatever aspect about yourself you wish to emphasize particularly. The heading 'Other details' serves much the same purpose, where it completes the picture and reveals more of your personal side and interests. Try to avoid listing numerous sporting activities which you pursue infrequently.

☞ **5.** The most common presentation is on A4 size paper. It's ordinary and conventional though, so you're not obliged to stick to it when applying to the more 'trendy' sectors such as advertising or public relations.

Nicole Turner
10 Lavander Road
Manchester
051-381 54725

C.V. personalized → SECRETARY WP WORD 5.1

QUALIFICATIONS

Jan–Mar 1992: Course in Word Processing Wordperfect 5.1 and keyboard skills. Retraining in office management skills 430 hours. Institute of Secretarial Training, Manchester.

June 1965: Diploma in shorthand/typing at the Office Centre, Manchester.

good use of spacing.

WORK EXPERIENCE

1972 - 1980: <u>Secretary shorthand-typist</u>. Driving School, Main St, Manchester.
  – Registering students, filing dossiers (200 per year)
  – Customer relations (training in Highway Code)
  – Secretarial duties
  – Experience of using Canon electronic typewriter

Setting out the most important aspects of the work.

1965 - 1972: <u>Database operator</u>. City Centre Arcade, Manchester.
  – Recording accounts (750 per month)
  – Administrative duties, supervision of 3 personnel, allocation of daily functions

OTHER DETAILS

Since 1980: Professional activity ceased while raising a family during which time I also acted as <u>Secretary to the Manchester Judo Club</u>.

Leisure Activities: Co-ordinator of workshop on painting on silks at the Manchester Women's Club. Swimming. Gardening.

Age 44. Married. 3 children (aged 23, 19, 8)
Driving licence. Car owner.

CONTENT: THE FIVE ESSENTIAL POINTS

☞ **1.** A CV is the record of your professional career. It's the passport to your first contact with a potential employer.

It supplies the basic material for a possible interview. It's the summary of all your skills, knowledge and experience and therefore merits special preparation. You need to be aware of the image you wish to convey to others. You should be careful to use terms which are clear and accessible to everyone.

☞ **2.** You are not obliged, if it's a very long one, to include your entire work history. You should only include the information relevant to the post that's to be filled. Therefore, leave out any details which will get you nowhere - don't hand over the rope with which to hang yourself. The important thing is to catch the employer's attention and he's more likely to be attentive if you share a mutual interest.

☞ **3.** The stumbling block par excellence has to be the question of pay. Resist all temptation to bring it up in your CV. The question of pay is discussed between both parties concerned and is dependent on many diverse factors. It is certain to come up during the interview so know your 'market value' beforehand. Find out the going rate. Look up your old contacts or friends who are working and seek advice from the local grapevine. Location has its part to play in the decision – in general the larger the town the larger the salary.

☞ **4.** Go into detail when describing past occupations, your level of knowledge of foreign languages and the content (within reason) of any training courses you've completed. You need to highlight your personal talents and skills as much as your professional know-how.

☞ **5.** The sequence of the headings 'Qualifications' and 'Work Experience' is a matter of personal choice. It largely depends on whichever order will show you in the best light, and also, of course, on your age.

At this point what is the more powerful selling point in your application, experience or qualifications? You could always refer to in-house training courses of more than a month's duration as experience.

> **HERE IS A COPY OF NICOLE'S CV. WE HAVE MADE NOTES ON OUR OBSERVATIONS CONCERNING ITS CONTENT**

Nicole Turner
10 Lavander Road
Manchester
051-381 54725

SECRETARY WP WORD 5.1

QUALIFICATIONS

Jan-Mar 1992: Course in Word Processing Wordperfect 5.1 and keyboard skills. Retraining in office management skills 430 hours. Institute of Secretarial Training, Manchester.

June 1965: Diploma in shorthand/typing at the Office Centre, Manchester.

WORK EXPERIENCE

1972 - 1980: <u>Secretary shorthand-typist</u>. Driving School, Main St, Manchester.
- Registering students, filing dossiers (200 per year)
- Customer relations (training in Highway Code)
- Secretarial duties
- Experience of using Canon electronic typewriter

1965 - 1972: <u>Database operator</u>. City Centre Arcade, Manchester.
- Recording accounts (750 per month)
- Administrative duties, supervision of 3 personnel, allocation of daily functions

[handwritten note: Stating figures makes for a concrete argument.]

[handwritten note: Good definition of post held.]

OTHER DETAILS

Since 1980: Professional activity ceased while raising a family during which time I also acted as <u>Secretary to the Manchester Judo Club</u>.

Leisure Activities: Co-ordinator of workshop on painting on silks at the Manchester Women's Club. Swimming. Gardening.

Age 44. Married. 3 children (aged 23, 19, 8)
Driving licence. Car owner.

[handwritten note: Highlights outside work activities.]

DRAWING UP A CV

IDENTIFICATION DETAILS

PHOTO
(optional)

POST APPLIED FOR

WORK EXPERIENCE

- Year   Name of Company
           Title of position held
           Description of duties
- Year   Name of Company
           Title of position held
           Description of duties

QUALIFICATIONS

– Year	Diploma	Establishment (optional)
– Year	specialized training	Number of hours
– Year	In-house training	Number of hours
– Foreign languages	level	
– Knowledge of software programmes		

OTHER DETAILS

- Leisure activities
- Sports
- Driver's licence + car

COMPILE YOUR OWN CV

WORK EXPERIENCE

QUALIFICATIONS

OTHER DETAILS

AND ABOVE ALL
DON'T FORGET

TO USE POSITIVE ACTION WORDS

Acted – Assembled – Analyzed
Calculated – Coordinated – Commu-
nicated – Created
Delegated – Designed – Developed –
Diagnosed – Displayed
Instructed – Implemented
Motivated
Operated – Organized
Participated – Programmed
Recorded
Sold – Supervised

TO BE EXPLICIT UNDER THE HEADING
'OTHER DETAILS'

You only need to mention a few outside of work activities if you practise
them regularly. You should be in a
position to discuss them in some depth.
Refer to a variety of activities, both
individual and collective, such as
reading and a team activity such as
basketball for example.

TO LIST

Be precise. For each previous job
specify numbers (of clients, cases...),
with whom, for what purpose...

Section 6
LETTER WRITING

SELF-ASSESSMENT QUESTIONNAIRE

Let's check your technique for composing letters of application. Reply spontaneously to the following questions.

	YES	NO
Even after 20 letters, I still spend a lot of time composing each one	☐	☐
I don't always specify the name of the person I'm writing to	☐	☐
I don't say much about myself in the letter	☐	☐
I always spend ages composing the introduction	☐	☐
I use at least two of these formulas:	☐	☐

– I wish to...   – I'm looking for...
– I look forward to...   – In the hope of hearing...

	YES	NO
I only ever write one paragraph	☐	☐
To save time, I photocopy a good letter	☐	☐
I copy a model from a book	☐	☐
I get somebody else to write it for me because my handwriting isn't very impressive	☐	☐
I don't advertise in the 'Wanted' ads section, I don't think it's very effective or worthwhile	☐	☐

TOTAL [   ]

····· **ANALYSIS OF RESULTS**

1 - 3 'YES'

You are avoiding the common pitfalls and are on the right track.

If you read over our tips then your letters may be even more productive. Compose a couple of rough copies and examine them for possibilities of inserting a few more personal phrases.

3 - 6 'YES'

Watch out! You tend to overlook the importance of written correspondence. Even if your CV is very good, it's the covering letter which gives the employer the desire to look at it.

Work through the entire chapter. Write a standard letter and adapt it according to whoever it's aimed at.

More than 6 'YES'

Written correspondence isn't exactly your strong point. Follow our step-by-step advice and then examine the letter plan.

NOW IT'S YOUR TURN!

THE GOLDEN RULES FOR WRITING YOUR LETTER OF APPLICATION

PERSONALIZE YOUR LETTER-WRITING

– By naming the person it's destined for (find out beforehand).

– By talking about yourself. What assets can you bring to the job? Who are you? What can you do?

– By not copying model letters from books.

– By composing a different letter for each individual post.

– By paying attention to the look of the letter. A good visual presentation gets noticed.

– The envelope is also an important, often overlooked, detail so treat it with the same care.

BE CONVINCING

– Keep your sentences simple and to the point. Don't borrow other people's formulas.

– Always proofread – the slightest spelling mistake will eliminate you from the short list of applicants.

– Don't get a third party to write it for you – even if a graphologist is going to analyze it. You have no idea what an employer may base his decision on.

– Grammatically speaking, avoid use of the conditional tense (I would...if) and the passive voice (I was seen to be...). Be positive and use the present tense (I do, I am).

WRITING IS A GOOD THING... BUT HAVE YOU EVER CONSIDERED ADVERTISING YOURSELF?

John TURNER
10 Lavander Road
Manchester

Telephone number missing — always a useful thing.

30 March 1993

Mr Daniel Moran
ARVAC & CO
8 Beaver Avenue
Manchester

Bonus point ! Personalize your letters.

Dear Sir,

I was greatly interested by your advertisement in the 'New Factory' of 23 March.

Introduction short but to the point.

Description a little too brief. What are the strong points of this application?

My many years of experience have enabled me to master the most modern techniques in the fields of electronics and computers, as well as allowing me to develop leadership skills (heading a team of 20 personnel). I feel this post as Department Head suits me perfectly.

A good formula, don't wait for further reply but suggest an interview.

A future interview would give me the opportunity to elaborate on the contents of my CV which I enclose. My desired salary scale is in the region of £26,000 per annum.

Yours faithfully,

John Turner

John Turner

LETTER PLAN

THREE MAIN PARAGRAPHS

1st Paragraph

☞ TO CAPTURE THE INTEREST OF THE READER

The opening phrase should be original enough to give the reader a desire to continue reading. Think of the employer's needs? What do you know about him/her?

In the case of a reply to an ad, be as brief as possible:
- what ad?
- what source?
- what date?

2nd Paragraph

☞ A BRIEF AND CONCISE INTRODUCTION TO YOURSELF. WHO AM I? WHAT DO I HAVE TO OFFER?

A short but clear synopsis of your suitability for the post.

What aspects of the job interest you and why? What have you already achieved?

3rd Paragraph

☞ ASKING FOR AN INTERVIEW AND SUITABLE ENDING

Propose an interview. Mention your expectations as regards salary (if this is required) and end with a suitable form of address.

A FEW TIPS

☞ YOU HAVE NO EXPERIENCE. Highlight your qualifications and any skills you have developed in personal activities.

☞ YOU DON'T HAVE THE DIPLOMA OR THE LEVEL REQUIRED. Don't dwell on this point, talk instead of your experience.

☞ YOU ARE OLDER THAN THE REQUIREMENT STATED IN THE AD. Convey instead your dynamic and resourceful personality.

☞ YOU ARE HANDICAPPED BY YOUR HANDWRITING. Your handwriting is very important. Make your handwriting as clear as possible. If necessary use a word processor at all times and print when this is not possible.

☞ YOU ARE BY NATURE A WORRIER AND A PESSIMIST. Try to use only positive vocabulary and proofread to eliminate negative statements.

☞ DON'T SAY: It would be a great honour – In the hope that... – Unemployed for 2 years – I await...

☞ DO SAY: I'm applying for the job because... – An interview would give me an opportunity to... – Available immediately – At your convenience....

YOUR LIFELINE

YOU REPLY TO A JOB ADVERTISEMENT.
COMPLETE THE THREE PARAGRAPHS OF THE LETTER BY COMPOSING TWO SENTENCES
PER PARAGRAPH.

1st Paragraph
☞ I noted with interest your ad which appeared...
☞ Your ad which appeared in the *Guardian* of the ... attracted my attention and prompts me to offer my skills for your consideration.

Your turn...

2nd Paragraph
☞ My five years' experience has permitted me to master several WP programmes.
☞ I was thus able to develop my organizational skills and leadership qualities in creating a customer service section.
☞ These are the skills which I could offer your company.

Your turn...

3rd Paragraph
☞ I would be happy to provide further details during the course of a future interview. Yours faithfully...

Your turn...

YOUR LETTER

COMPOSE A FIRST SAMPLE OF A LETTER OF APPLICATION. HAVE A COMPETENT PERSON PROOFREAD AND CORRECT IT.

Section 7
THE JOB INTERVIEW

TEST

If the phrase corresponds to your usual mode of behaviour, place an X in the column marked 'yes', if not mark the 'no' column. If you're in the process of looking for your first job, reply while imagining your probable behaviour.

QUESTIONS	YES	NO
1 Before the interview I identify all the positive attributes that favour me for the position.	....	....
2 I find out all I can in advance about the role of the people I'll be meeting at interview.	....	....
3 I ask questions during the interview.	....	....
4 I try to find out the reason why this vacancy has arisen.	....	....
5 I find out all I can about the future of the business: turnover figures, objectives, competition.	....	....
6 Before the interview, I know the current market value of the post.	....	....
7 I know how to present my reasons for leaving previous companies or organizations in a favourable light.	....	....
8 I know how to convey my motivation and aptitude for the post.	....	....
9 I can briefly list the advantages that my appointment would bring to the company.	....	....
10 On leaving the interview, I would know how to calculate its outcome.	....	....

ADD UP THE TOTAL OF YES SCORES

ANALYSIS OF RESULTS

The interview is the final and most important obstacle in your path to a job: you have to convince the recruiter that you are the person he is looking for. The test which you have just completed allows you to assess your performance at interview, as each phrase describes a particular facet of your behaviour, a systematic attitude or action.

To be read on completion of the self-assessment sheet

Calculate your results

☞ *Less than 5 'yes' responses*

You don't carry out the necessary preparation before your interview, you have no definite objectives and you fail to project a sufficiently dynamic image of yourself. You'll have to work a lot harder to convince your interviewers. Pay particular attention to this chapter.

☞ *Between 5 and 8 'yes' responses*

There is room for improvement. You're not forceful enough. You need to build up your self-confidence and ensure plenty of preparation before an interview.

☞ *More than 8 'yes' responses*

You are in control of the basic interview survival techniques. Do not, however, underestimate the importance of the advice to follow in this chapter. It's not enough to show that you're good, you have to prove that you're the best person for the job.

BEFORE THE INTERVIEW

GETTING AN INTERVIEW BY PHONE

You have decided on a likely company to approach and you'd like to get in touch with the Head of Personnel. Or maybe you've come across a tempting ad in the paper which gives a telephone number. So here you are by the phone. Before making the call, take time to gather your thoughts and remember this rule.

THE SOLE PURPOSE OF THIS PHONE CALL IS TO OBTAIN AN INTERVIEW

On the phone, all you want to do is arrange an interview. Pure and simple it may sound but this requires a great effort on your part. The recruiter you'll be speaking to doesn't want to waste time interviewing the wrong person. He's going to want to find out whether or not you fit the profile he has in mind. You may keep finding yourself in this situation and it's you in particular who has everything to lose. It is worthwhile, therefore, preparing your answers in advance so you can convince the recruiter that you are the one he needs. Remember, you won't have time to ascertain exactly what is foremost in his mind. To get around this problem, get straight to the point. Focus the conversation on the arrangement of an interview.

A FEW TIPS
– Introduce yourself.
– Ask for an interview. 'Your company really interests me. I'm looking for a post in accounting and I saw your ad in this morning's *Guardian*. When could we meet? This afternoon or tomorrow morning?'
– Prepare a script beforehand, giving basic information about yourself and proposing an interview as soon as possible.
– Try to turn his objections or questions into grounds for interview: 'Do you have any experience?' 'It's difficult to go into detail over the phone. I could explain at greater length face to face. Could we meet this afternoon or perhaps tomorrow morning.'
– End the conversation as soon as you have obtained an interview, reiterating time and place of interview and the name of the person you've been speaking to. Ensure also that he has noted your name, address and phone number.

PREPARE YOUR TELEPHONE TECHNIQUE

Nicole, through her local JobCentre, was given a place on a word processing course. She now feels more in control of her situation. Her neighbour, Michelle, has tipped her off that the Head of Personnel where she works is looking for a secretary. She gives Nicole the phone number and tells her to call, mentioning her name. Before doing so, Nicole puts down on paper exactly what she is going to say.

IDENTIFY WHO YOU'RE SPEAKING TO	My name is Nicole Turner. Is that Mr Wright, Head of Personnel?
NAME A REFEREE	Michelle Martin, a neighbour of mine, gave me your phone number and told me that you were looking for a secretary. I'm very interested in the job.
JUSTIFY YOUR SUITABILITY FOR THE JOB	I'm an excellent typist and I also have experience of word processors. I am very enthusiastic
WHY YOU WANT THE JOB	I would really like to work in your company. My neighbour is very happy there. I hear it has a very friendly and busy atmosphere.
DIRECT APPROACH IN ASKING FOR INTERVIEW LEAVES NO ROOM FOR REFUSAL	When can I meet you? This afternoon or tomorrow perhaps?

NOW IT'S YOUR TURN TO COMPOSE YOUR SPEECH FOLLOWING THE ABOVE EXAMPLE

WHO WILL BE INTERVIEWING YOU?

Depending on the size of the company and the type of job on offer, you may meet one or several interviewers. Know who they are to find the best way of communicating with them. The recruiter you will meet may be:

AN OUTSIDE CONSULTANT

A consultant from a professional recruitment agency or an agency for temporary employment, for example. His function is to draw up a short list of applicants who fulfil the requirements of the job. His fee will be based on a percentage of the annual salary in question. He will be just as thorough in his efforts to offer his client (the company) a high quality service. If he is satisfied, he will in turn pass on your application to...

A RECRUITMENT SPECIALIST WITHIN THE COMPANY

He is a member of the personnel department. His function is to examine applications on the basis of the needs of the company, for a particular department or service. His objective will be to ensure that your personality will fit into the office culture and the company's long-term objectives. If he is satisfied, he will in turn pass on your application to...

YOUR FUTURE BOSS

He is of course your most immediate concern. He is the instigator of the whole job offer process. He will want to confirm your qualifications and decide whether you will get on with one another. He may not be the only one who wants to meet you, especially if the post means a lot of contact with others.

GATHER MORE INFORMATION

Look out for useful information of the type that your interviewer might neglect to give you. In particular:

☞ the financial state of the business, its current and future markets; find out from such sources as the Chamber of Commerce, the competition, suppliers and sub-contractors;

☞ the current market value of the post in other businesses belonging to the same activity sector, in order to be able to negotiate your eventual salary; telephone professional associations and unions.

TYPICAL OUTLINE OF AN INTERVIEW

1. MAKING CONTACT	– Identifying both parties
	– Agreement on the purpose of the interview
2. DISCUSSING THE BUSINESS AND THE POST	– The interviewer explains
	– The applicant probes
3. THE APPLICANT'S SKILLS AND APTITUDES	– The interviewer asks
	– The applicant explains
4. THE APPLICANT'S MOTIVATION	– The interviewer explores
	– The applicant convinces
5. PAY	– Both parties negotiate
6. CONCLUSION	– Each party gives an indication of the outcome of the interview.

DEFINE YOUR OBJECTIVES

Carefully determine your **objectives**, the results that you hope to gain from this interview. The following table proposes some essential objectives as well as the **methods** necessary to achieve them.

OBJECTIVES

1. *To reaffirm* or invalidate your being chosen as a candidate. You're still lacking certain information that is necessary to make an informed decision. You are expecting the interviewer to supply it.

2. *To reassure the recruiter*, and show him that you are responsible, dynamic, self-reliant and friendly.

3. *To convince the interviewer* that your skills, personality and motivation correspond exactly to those necessary for the post being offered.

4. *To obtain the best possible salary*. Take into account all that you have to offer as well as the going rate for the particular post.

5. To know *what decisions* will be made following the interview, how you will inform the recruiter of your decision to continue or withdraw your application, and how you will be notified of the decision reached by the company.

METHODS NECESSARY TO ACHIEVE THESE OBJECTIVES

1. *Active listening*. Asking pertinent questions, making sure that you understand all information given and persisting in finding out all details which are important to you.

2. *Your behaviour during the course of the interview* will prove it. You pose well thought out questions, you prove that you're dynamic by taking the initiative and sometimes leading the interview, you know how to listen well and you handle all questioning with assurance.

3. *Assert yourself*, dealing with each point mentioned in the advertisement, one by one. In order to convince the interviewer, emphasize your experience and cite facts and figures where possible.

4. *Negotiate*, using the classic methods of negotiation (see page 89).

5. Don't leave the interview before gaining *a clear and specific reply*.

MY PRIMARY OBJECTIVES

PREPARE YOUR QUESTIONS

It's important to do your homework before the interview so prepare your questions about the company by writing them out.
You could base your questions on the following:

QUESTIONS ABOUT THE COMPANY
– Is it a market leader in its sector?
– Growth:
   number of employees
   turnover
   position in the market
   outlook
– Organization: organogram
  (an organization chart)

QUESTIONS ABOUT THE VACANCY
– Reason for the vacancy:
   creation of a post, why?
   replacing somebody, was this person replaced or have they actually left the company?
– Superiors
– Opportunity for taking initiative
– Means available
– Communication lines
– Possibilities for external contacts
– Growth potential of the post
– Essential duties
– Particular demands and problems
– Salary

QUESTIONS ABOUT COMPANY POLICY CONCERNING PERSONNEL
– Internal mobility (possibilities for promotion)
– Training opportunities
– Salary policies
– Methods for recognition of particular results

MY QUESTIONS

TYPICAL INTERVIEW QUESTIONS

No matter what type of interview situation you may find yourself in, the interviewer is bound to touch on three main areas:

☞ Your professional qualifications
☞ Your motivation
☞ Your personality

YOUR QUALIFICATIONS

Tell me about your previous related experience
What posts have you held?
What can you do?
What aspect of the job do you prefer?
What were your reasons for leaving previous jobs?
What are your future career plans?
What's your impression of the job on offer?
Why will you succeed?

YOUR MOTIVATION

Why are you here?
What are your interests outside work?
What do you know about this company?
How long have you been looking for work?

YOUR PERSONALITY

Who are you?
What are your personal strengths and weaknesses?
Do you like responsibility and why?

PREPARE YOUR ANSWERS

Train yourself to give sharp, well-formed responses. In particular to the following three questions:

1. WHAT INTERESTS YOU ABOUT PROFESSIONAL LIFE?

2. WHAT ARE YOUR PERSONAL STRENGTHS AND WEAKNESSES?

3. WHAT WOULD THIS COMPANY STAND TO GAIN BY EMPLOYING YOU?

DURING THE INTERVIEW

MAKE THE INTERVIEWER TALK

Don't allow the interview to turn into an interrogation session. In this situation the interviewer is firing questions at you and you are answering them until little by little you become the accused party, obliged to constantly defend yourself. Even if you do so brilliantly, you are on the losing side.
Why?

- Because you are learning nothing new, about the company, the vacancy or your interviewer. Nothing that will help you to make an informed decision.
- You will give the impression that you are a passive person, lacking in motivation. At no time do you take the initiative or show a spark of interest.
- Most importantly, you do not discover the intentions of your interviewer, you can't possibly come up with a means of convincing him if you don't know where he's coming from.

Get off to the right start by making the interviewer do the talking. Perhaps he will do so anyway, in which case you should punctuate the dialogue with pertinent questions which will enable you to glean relevant points of information for any negotiations later on. If the interviewer begins the interview by questioning you about your past and the contents of your CV, ask him instead to reply to your questions first concerning the post and the company. Explain your request by saying that you need this information in order to make your own decision.

REASSURE HIM

As a general rule, an interviewer needs to be reassured. He can't afford to make a mistake any more than you can. Imagine the cost of appointing the wrong person to the job: three months' salary (with national insurance contributions) + the cost of setting in motion the entire recruitment process yet again (often the equivalent of one or two months' salary) + the time necessary to train a new employee. The interviewer thus needs to be completely reassured as to your skills, potential and motivation.

YOUR SKILLS

You have to prove to him that you fulfil the stated requirements of the post. Grand, airy declarations are not enough, you need more concrete proof by citing solid facts to back up these declarations. For example: 'I have shown myself to be capable of taking the initiative. I replaced my supervisor when he was out on sick leave for six months. The Managing Director expressed his complete satisfaction: department objectives were reached and even surpassed by 20 per cent'.

YOUR MOTIVATION

The recruiter has to find out whether or not you are solidly committed to the job. Speak openly, illustrating your steadfast approach to building up your career, realizing your ambitions and reaching your objectives.

Your motivation increases as you gain experience and you know that firm resolution is necessary in order to keep on reaching your objectives. Show yourself to be both ambitious and pragmatic.

YOUR POTENTIAL

The company is looking for somebody who will remain with them for 5, 10 or possibly 20 years. In the case of candidates being equally well-qualified for the post, they will opt for the one who appears to have the capacity to develop and adapt to the company's requirements. In other words, the interviewer is going to try to discover your 'potential', the personal qualities which will benefit the company in the long term: initiative, flexibility, creativity, ability to learn, sense of endeavour, capacity to lead and motivate others . . . seize the opportunity to list all your positive characteristics.

TALK POSITIVELY ABOUT YOURSELF

This exercise is aimed at training you to speak positively about yourself. Many people automatically emphasize their difficulties and failures, and not their positive qualities and successes. This leads them, often wrongly, to convey a negative image of themselves. This must be avoided in an interview.

INSTRUCTIONS
Rewrite each of the following responses in order to make them sound more positive. Example: 'Do you speak French?' – 'No, French was never my strong point at school and I've never used it since.' You can say almost the same thing while presenting a better image of yourself by avoiding the negative terminology. Example: 'I studied French to O level and I can understand correspondence and follow a conversation. A supplementary course over a couple of weeks would enable me to gain a degree of fluency in spoken French.'

EXERCISE 1
Interviewer: 'Can you use a computer?'
Candidate: 'It would be misleading to answer yes. I did complete a course in WP with my previous company, but that was five years ago, the programme is now obsolete, and I only used it for a month. I have to admit that I have forgotten how to operate it'.

YOUR REPLY:

EXERCISE 2
Interviewer: 'Why were you let go from your previous job?'
Candidate: 'Well, the new boss couldn't stand me. He wanted to put one of his former colleagues in my place. I'm just not the sort of person who could fight back. He harassed me to such an extent that I made a few silly mistakes and he pounced on the opportunity to get rid of me.'

YOUR REPLY:

NEGOTIATING YOUR SALARY

This area of the interview is useful, even essential but it is also delicate. So delicate in fact that many people avoid it and accept without a murmur whatever conditions are imposed upon them by the employer.

Three tips for successful negotiation:

1. Lead the employer to make his proposal and then declare your target figure.
It's a tactical advantage to have the interviewer propose a figure. This allows you to modify your position. If their proposal is greater than you expected then you can adjust your sights a little higher. On the other hand, if it's less than you were hoping for, you have a little more time to negotiate.
Whatever happens, it's imperative that you have some idea of the going rate for the particular post in the job market.
Whatever additional extras you can offer the company justify an increase in salary or other perks. Once you've done your homework and have a fixed salary in mind, you should also bear in mind these two tips on how to formulate your demand:
– suggest a salary scale rather than a fixed figure. This gives you room to negotiate within this scale towards the higher figure;
– justify your demand by emphasizing the additional knowledge and expertise you can offer the company. This gives you greater scope for negotiation.

2. Where there is a difference of opinion, explore the alternatives:
You are asking for more than the recruiter can and wants to offer. If the difference is too great, then obviously this post is not for you. You will have to make a decision.
If the difference is a 'reasonable' one, then try to find other means of compensation or a path towards a compromise. Compensation could take many varied forms: status (executive), extra holidays, guaranteed promotion, further training programmes, company car, etc. Look for benefits which the company can easily offer you.

3. Formulate a premise for reaching an agreement. The best outcome is for both parties to benefit from the settlement. Each party gains some concession they were hoping for and forgoes something less important.

BE PREPARED FOR NEGOTIATION

For the position which interests you, calculate:

1. THE AVERAGE GOING RATE FOR THIS POST IN A COMPANY OF SIMILAR SIZE

2. YOUR PROJECTED SALARY AND WHY?

3. THE SALARY SCALE YOU INTEND TO ANNOUNCE

   from:

   to:

4. POSSIBLE CONCESSIONS

CLASSIC INTERVIEW PITFALLS
SELF-ASSESSMENT

What would you do in the following situations? Choose your reply from among the three we've proposed. Afterwards check the commentary.

1. THE INTERVIEWER SETS THE BALL ROLLING BY QUESTIONING YOU ON YOUR CV

   a) You reply as accurately as possible. ☐

   b) You explain that you would first like to find out more about the company. ☐

   c) You refuse to be 'submitted to this interrogation'. ☐

2. THE INTERVIEWER DOUBTS THE SINCERITY OF WHAT YOU SAY

   a) You ask him the reason for his doubts. ☐

   b) You decide that this interview is pointless. ☐

   c) You strive to be more convincing. ☐

3. THE INTERVIEWER ASKS YOU ABOUT YOUR PRIVATE LIFE

   a) You tell him it's none of his business. ☐

   b) You say as little as possible in reply. ☐

   c) You try to laugh it off. ☐

4. THE INTERVIEWER BIDS YOU SIT DOWN AND SAYS: 'RIGHT, I'M LISTENING...'

   a) You talk about yourself and your qualities. ☐

   b) You express your expectations of the interview. ☐

   c) You question him about the company. ☐

5. IT LOOKS AS THOUGH THE INTERVIEWER IS GETTING BORED

   a) You continue unperturbed. ☐

   b) You say something to regain his attention. ☐

   c) You let him know you think so. ☐

COMMENTARY

To be read after replying to the self-assessment test on the classic pitfalls of the interview

1.

    a) You're missing out on an opportunity to state your expectations of this interview;

    b) Well done, you display a sense of independence and responsibility;

    c) You're getting off on the wrong foot with your interviewer, by attributing to him attitudes that he probably never had.

2.

    a) You force the interviewer to specify exactly what's on his mind. This gives you time to prepare your reply and identify the problem;

    b) Don't get annoyed. Perhaps it's the interviewer's intention to provoke you and make you fly off the handle. If this is the case then you're helping him to succeed;

    c) If in spite of your further explanations, the doubt still persists, then perhaps its source lies elsewhere, so ask him.

3.

    a) Try not to reply in an aggressive fashion. You'll make him wonder why you are so defensive;

    b) Rather than giving a flustered reply, simply ask him why he's questioning you on such an area;

    c) The best way to handle such provocation.

4.

    a) No, don't start selling yourself without knowing what the interviewer is looking for, you run the risk of error;

    b) You've passed the first test with flying colours. You've reaffirmed your application and given a framework to the interview;

    c) You've set off to discover more about your interviewer, a good start which will allow you to modify your behaviour and arguments to fit in with his expectations.

5.

    a) OK. So you don't allow yourself to be disconcerted but by not changing your attitude you risk making the situation even worse;

    b) Watch the effect this has; if it doesn't work, then the reason for his attitude lies elsewhere;

    c) You've chosen the most effective measure: get him to give you the reason for his disinterest. You are forcing him to sit up and notice you again.

A POSSIBLE INTERVIEW ROUTE

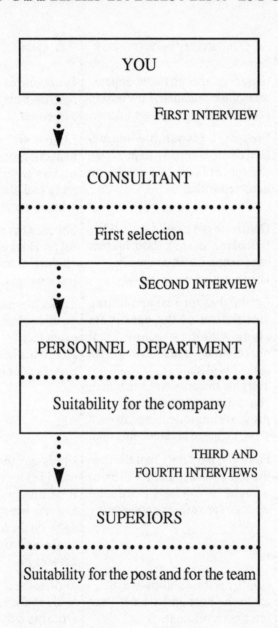

YOU

FIRST INTERVIEW

CONSULTANT

First selection

SECOND INTERVIEW

PERSONNEL DEPARTMENT

Suitability for the company

THIRD AND
FOURTH INTERVIEWS

SUPERIORS

Suitability for the post and for the team

REVIEW TABLE

INTERVIEW PROCESS	A COMPETENT INTERVIEWER	A COMPETENT CANDIDATE
MAKING CONTACT	Observes the physical appearance of the candidate, how he presents himself, his self-confidence.	Is in control of his nerves, and reaffirms his determination and objectives.
PRESENTATION OF THE POSITION ON OFFER AND THE COMPANY	Presents a favourable impression of the company to motivate the candidate's desire to be involved with it.	Listens attentively, asks pertinent questions. Shows an interest in the company and his sense of responsibility as regards his application.
SKILLS AND APTITUDES	Confirms the candidate's skills by making him talk about his past experience, based on the CV. Discovers his weak points.	Focuses his replies on successful previous experiences. Highlights his personal and professional assets.
REAL MOTIVES OF THE APPLICANT	Establishes the real and lasting motivation of the candidate along with his psychological make-up by questioning him about his plans. Tests his sincerity and strength of character by putting him under pressure, eg questioning him about a change in career direction.	Talks honestly, emphasizing positive elements and citing relevant facts. Keeps his head under provocative questioning.
SALARY	Finds out the salary that the candidate's looking for – clue to what he thinks he's worth and what he can offer the company.	Finds out the forecast budget provided for the post. Reaffirms his own value. Gets the interviewer to agree and settle on the top end of the salary scale and on other financial advantages.
CONCLUSION	Confirms the candidate's interest in the post and tries to secure a commitment.	Verifies the interviewer's interest in his application. Obtains a distinct idea of the notification procedure.

FINAL POINT

Actively seeking employment is a full-time job in itself. You can't expect to get anywhere, certainly not to interview stage, by dashing off a mere two or three letters a week. Nicole Turner finally found the secretarial post she'd been hoping for. Her notebook, in which she'd recorded all the statistics regarding her job search revealed the following figures: 163 applications sent off, 30 rejection letters, 16 interviews with potential employers, and the final outcome – a choice between two job offers.

You've read the book, so you have all the information you need on how to make your job search an effective one. Now all you need to do is organize it. Here are a few final tips:

DEVOTE TIME TO IT

Thirty-nine hours a week. Forget about other activities which will eat into this valuable time: doing up the bathroom, babysitting for your neighbour's children or learning Spanish. Stick to a timetable and make sure those around you respect it too. Better still, ask your nearest and dearest to help you keep to your arrangements.

DON'T GO IT ALONE

Take advantage of the stimulation and advice of other jobseekers. They could perhaps provide you with other leads you hadn't thought of. Agencies, JobCentres and your local career service regularly organize talks on job search techniques. Make regular appointments to meet with your Career Adviser at the JobCentre.

ORGANIZE YOUR SEARCH

Purchase a notebook or better still a folder and carefully record all the steps that you should or have already taken. Several methods of organization could prove useful:

- a notice board showing all your on spec applications, the dates of application, phone calls, and the response from the different companies;
- a synopsis of your replies to the small ads;
- a table recording all your moves, week after week, which allows you to offset results against the goals you set yourself.

GOOD LUCK ON THE ROAD TO EMPLOYMENT!